Backyard Bugs & Creepy-Crawlies

Dragonflies

Ashley Lee

Explore other books at:
WWW.ENGAGEBOOKS.COM

VANCOUVER, B.C.

ↄ WWW.ENGAGEBOOKS.COM

Dragonflies: Level 1
Backyard Bugs & Creepy Crawlies
Lee, Ashley 1995 –
Text © 2022 Engage Books
Design © 2022 Engage Books

Edited by: A.R. Roumanis

Text set in Epilogue

FIRST EDITION / FIRST PRINTING

LIBRARY AND ARCHIVES CANADA CATALOGUING IN PUBLICATION

Title: Dragonflies / Ashley Lee.
Names: Lee, Ashley, author.
Description: Series statement: Backyard bugs & creepy-crawlies
Engaging readers: level 1, beginner.

Identifiers: Canadiana (print) 20250448542 | Canadiana (ebook) 20250448569
ISBN 978-1-77878-705-8 (hardcover)
ISBN 978-1-77878-714-0 (softcover)

Subjects:
LCSH: Dragonflies—Juvenile literature.

Classification: LCC QL737.P94 C38 2025 | DDC J599.885—DC23

This project has been made possible in part by the Government of Canada.

Canada

Contents

What Are Dragonflies?

Dragonflies are one of the oldest flying insects. There are over 5,000 different kinds.

Dragonflies were on Earth before dinosaurs. They are about 300 million years old.

What Do Dragonflies Look Like?

Dragonflies have four wings. They stick straight out to the side.

Dragonflies have six legs. They can stand but they cannot walk.

Dragonflies have five eyes. They can see in almost all directions.

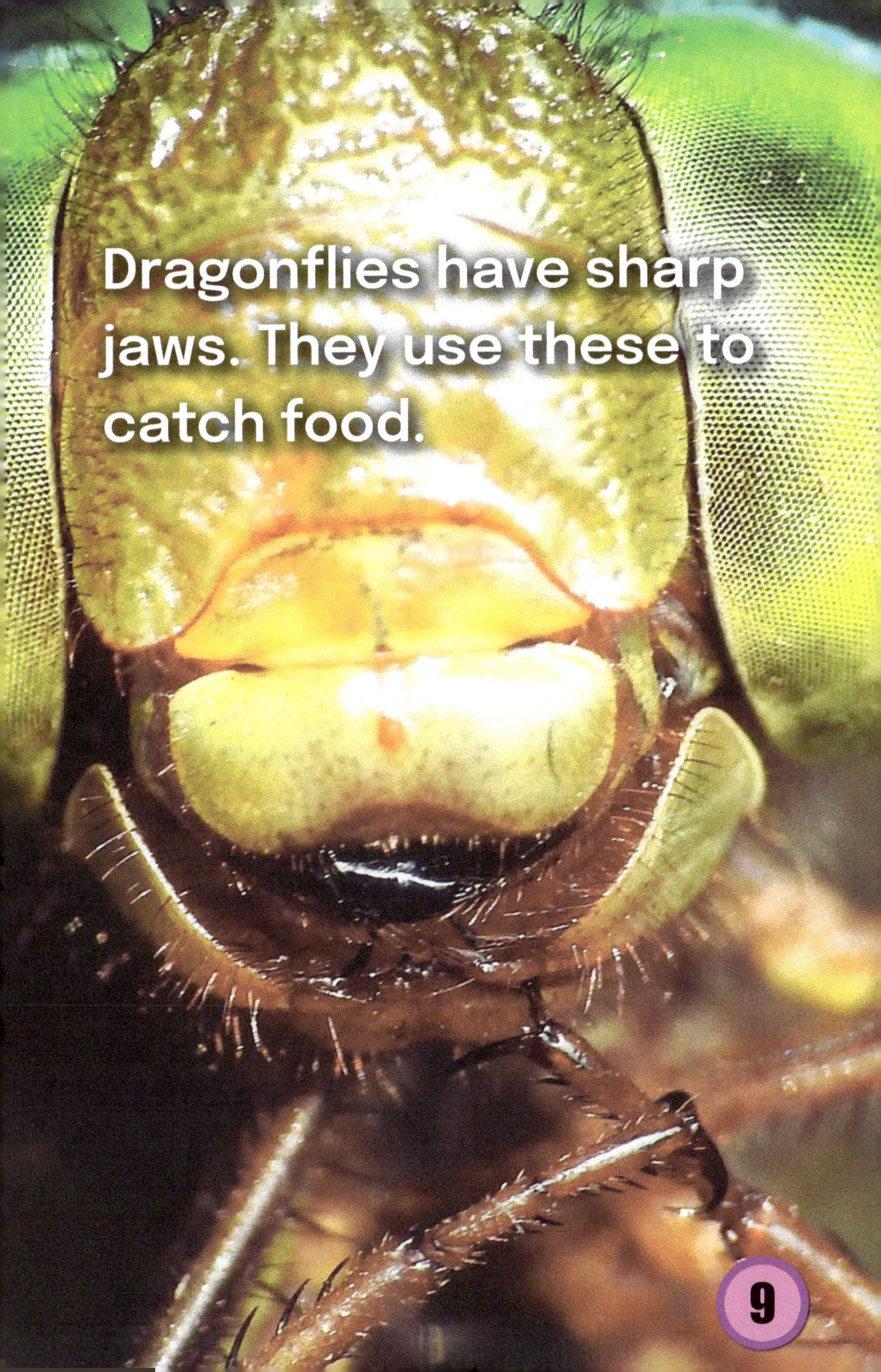

Dragonflies have sharp jaws. They use these to catch food.

Where Do Dragonflies Live?

Dragonflies live near fresh water. Fresh water is found in lakes, rivers, or ponds.

They live on every **continent** except Antarctica. It is too cold there.

Key Word

Continent: one of seven major areas of land on Earth.

10

What Do Dragonflies Eat?

Dragonflies eat other bugs. They like mosquitoes, flies, and butterflies.

One dragonfly can eat
hundreds of mosquitoes
in one day.

Dragonflies chase their **prey** while flying. They grab prey with their feet.

Dragonflies are better at catching food than any other animal.

Key Word

Prey: an animal that is hunted and eaten by another animal.

Dragonfly Behavior

Some dragonflies fly to warmer areas when the weather gets cold. This is called migration.

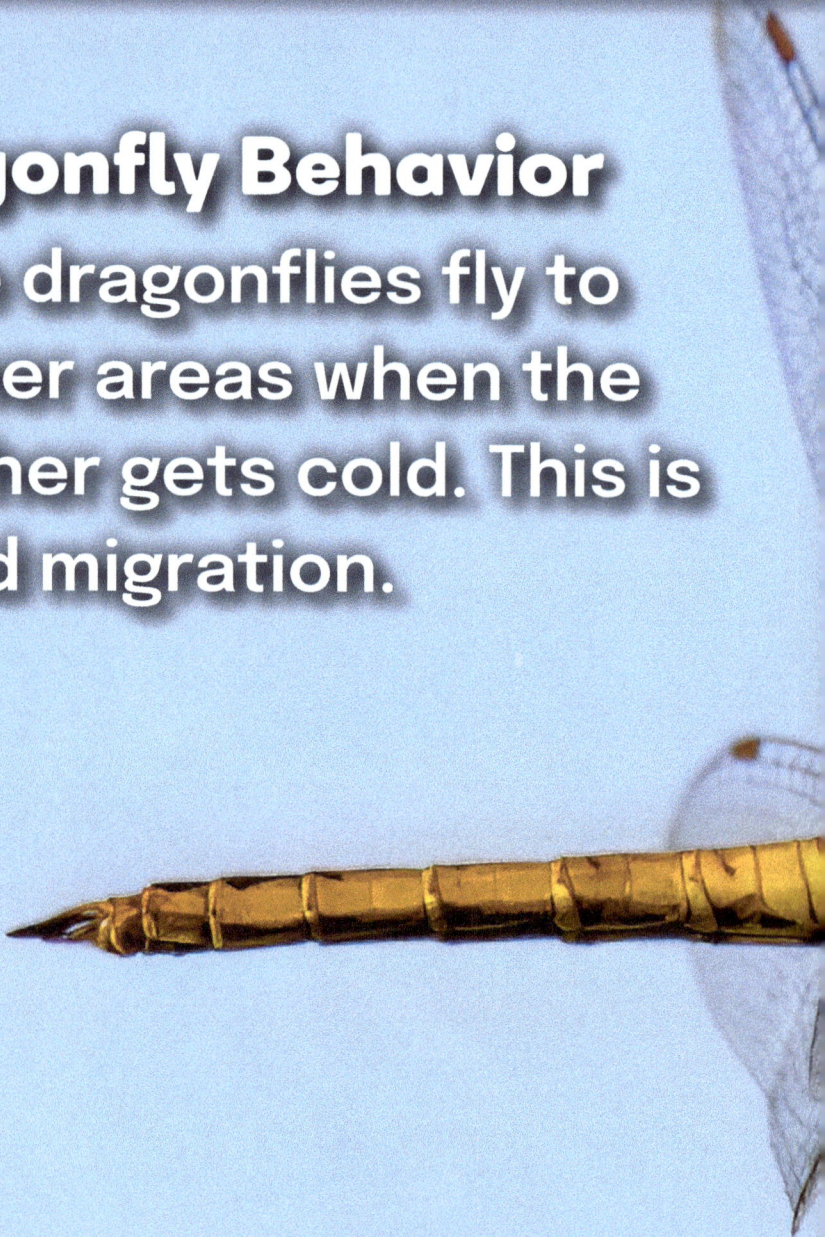

The globe skinner has the longest migration of any insect. They go back and forth across the Indian Ocean.

It is bad for dragonflies to get too hot. One way they cool themselves down is by obelisking.

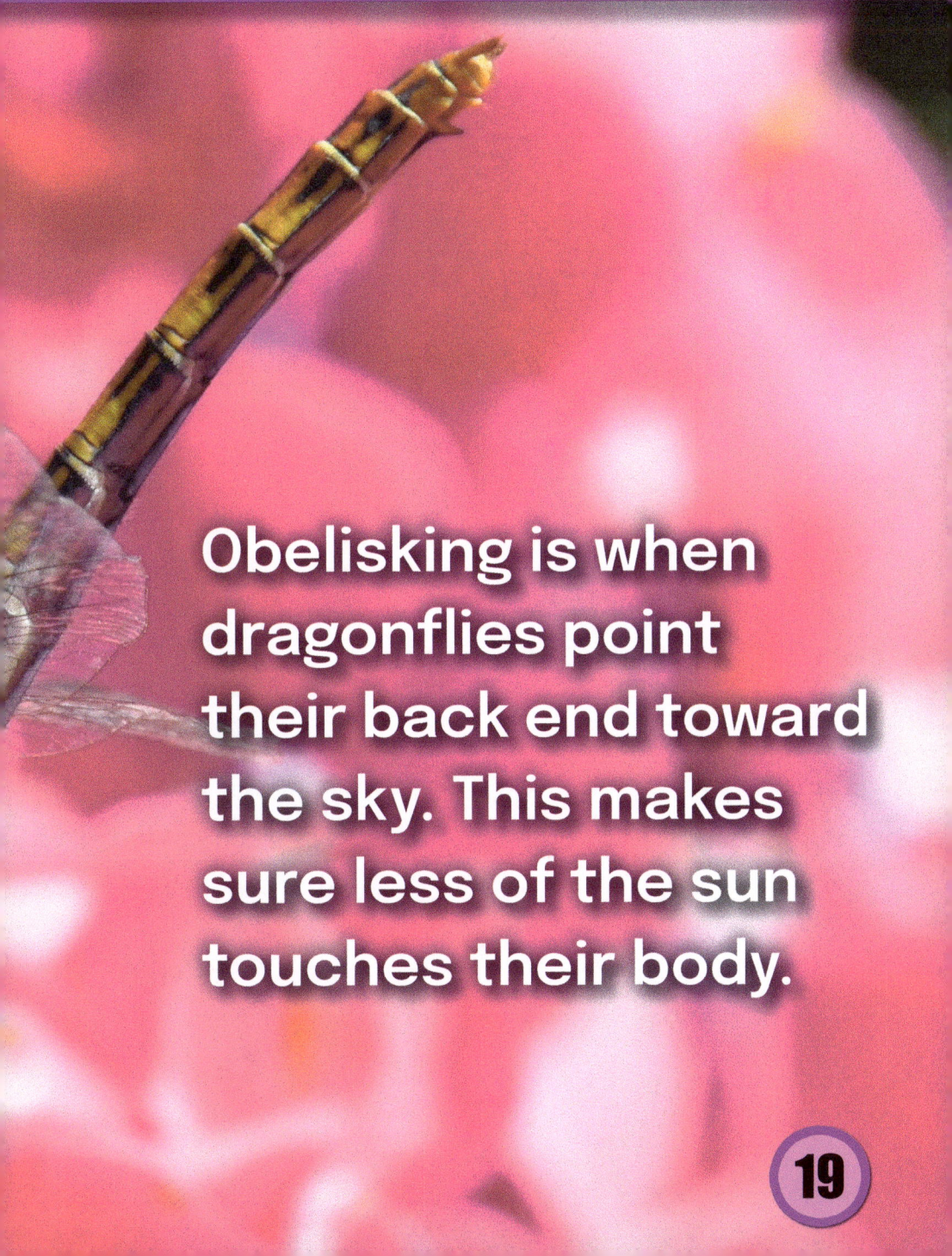

Obelisking is when dragonflies point their back end toward the sky. This makes sure less of the sun touches their body.

Dragonfly Life Cycle

Dragonflies lay eggs in water. Most eggs hatch in two to five weeks.

Young dragonflies are called larvae. Larvae live underwater.

Larvae leave the water when they are adults. They cannot fly far on their first flight.

Some dragonflies only live for a few weeks as adults. Others live up to a year.

Fun Facts

Larvae shed their skin to help them grow.

Dragonflies can fly backwards.

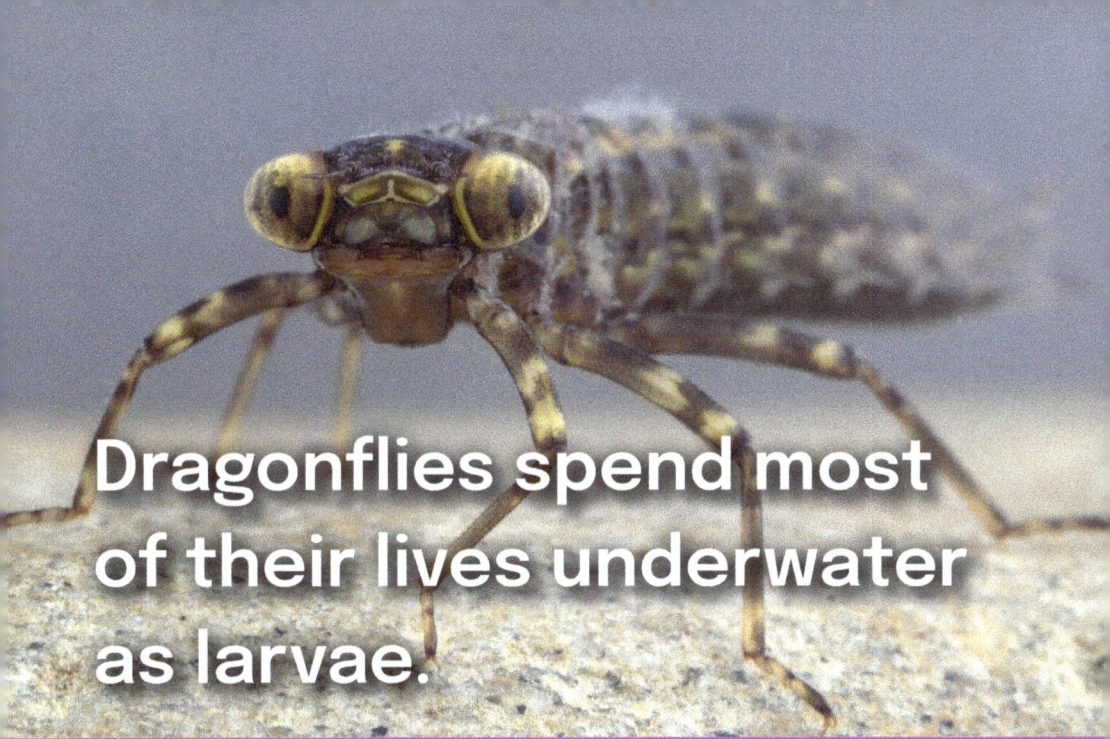

Dragonflies spend most of their lives underwater as larvae.

Dragonflies cannot fold their wings on top of their bodies.

Are Dragonflies Helpful or Harmful?

Dragonflies are helpful! Some mosquitoes carry diseases that can be passed to people.

Dragonflies eat these mosquitoes. This helps keep people safe.

Are Dragonflies in Danger?

Some kinds of dragonflies are dying out. They may soon be gone forever.

People are destroying their homes. This leaves dragonflies with nowhere to go.

29

Quiz

Test your knowledge of dragonflies by answering the following questions. The questions are based on what you have read in this book. The answers are listed on the bottom of the next page.

1 Were dragonflies on Earth before dinosaurs?

2 Can dragonflies walk?

3 Do dragonflies eat other bugs?

4 Is it bad for dragonflies to get too hot?

5 Do dragonflies lay eggs in water?

6 Can dragonflies fly backwards?

Explore other books in the
Backyard Bugs & Creepy Crawlies series!

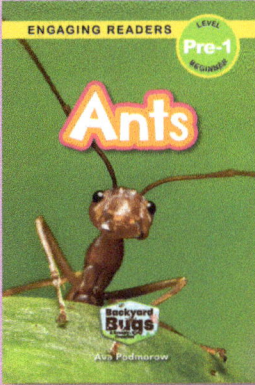

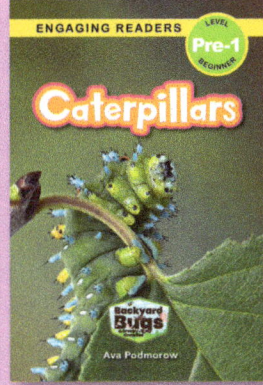

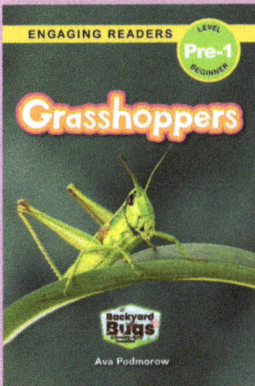

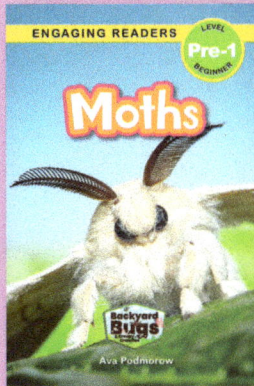

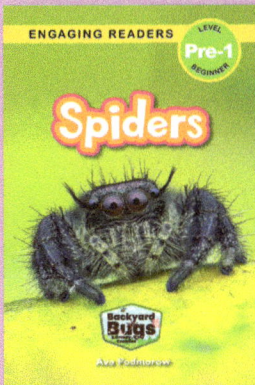

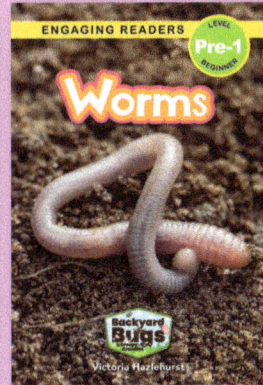

Visit www.engagebooks.com to explore more Engaging Readers.

www.ingramcontent.com/pod-product-compliance
Lightning Source LLC
Chambersburg PA
CBHW052035030426
42337CB00027B/5016